Note to Parents and Teachers

Dorling Kindersley Readers is a compelling new reading programme for children, designed in conjunction with leading literacy experts, including Cliff Moon M.Ed., Honorary Fellow of the University of Reading. Cliff Moon has spent many years as a teacher and teacher educator specializing in reading and has written more than 140 books for children and teachers. He reviews regularly for teachers' journals.

Beautiful illustrations and superb full-colour photographs combine with engaging, easy-to-read stories to offer a fresh approach to each subject. Each *Dorling Kindersley Reader* is guaranteed to capture a child's interest while developing his or her reading skills, general knowledge, and love of reading.

The four levels of *Dorling Kindersley Readers* are aimed at different reading abilities, enabling you to choose the books that are exactly right for each child:

Level 1 – Beginning to read
Level 2 – Beginning to read alone
Level 3 – Reading alone
Level 4 – Proficient readers

The "normal" age at which a child begins to read can be anywhere from three to eight years old, so these levels are intended only as a general guideline.

No matter which level you select, you can be sure that you are helping children learn to read, then read to learn!

LONDON, NEW YORK, MUNICH, PARIS
MELBOURNE, DELHI

Project Editor Carey Combe
Art Editor Mandy Earey

Senior Editor Linda Esposito
Senior Art Editor Diane Thistlethwaite
Production Melanie Downland
Picture Researcher Jamie Robertson
Picture Library Rachel Hilford,
Lee Thompson
Illustrator Chris Forsey

Reading Consultant
Cliff Moon M.Ed.

Published in Great Britain by
Dorling Kindersley Limited
80 The Strand, London WC2R 0RL
A Penguin Company

4 6 8 10 9 7 5 3

A CIP catalogue record for this book is available from
the British Library

ISBN 0-7513-2847-2

Colour reproduction by Colourscan, Singapore
Printed and bound in China by L Rex Printing Co., Ltd.

The publisher would like to thank the following for their kind permission
to reproduce their photographs.
a=above, b=below, c=centre, l=left, r=right, t=top.

AKG London: 8tl; Camera Press: 25tr, 25br, 25l; Corbis UK Ltd:
Bettmann 16bl; Robert Maas 39t; Dk Picture Library: 18l, 29c, 31br,
34/35; Mary Evans Picture Library: 9c; Galaxy Picture Library: Robin
Scagell 41tr; Ronald Grant Archive: EON Production 26tl, 26br;
Robert Harding Picture Library: Dusty Willison / International Stock
37t; Hulton Getty: 24tl, 27tr; Military Picture Library: Robin Adshead
31tl; PA News Photo Library: 17tr; Pictor International: 38b, 43br;
Rex Features: 30b, 31tl, 46/47; The Sun 47tr; Tripett 45t; Science
Photo Library: NRSC Ltd 42t; Frank Spooner Pictures: 21c, 23br;
Topham Picturepoint: 10br, 19tr, 22c, 35tr, 40b, 44b.

Jacket: Camera Press: John Philby Front cr; Corbis UK Ltd: Bettmann
Front cl; Pictor International: Back tl, Back tr; Rex Features: Front br.
All other images © Dorling Kindersley.
For further information see: www.dkimages.com

see our complete
catalogue at

Contents

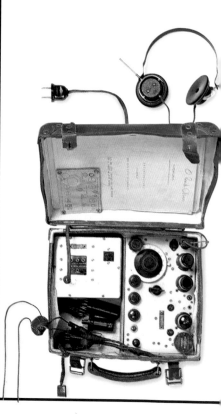

DK DORLING KINDERSLEY *READERS*

READING
3
ALONE

SPIES

Written by Richard Platt

A Dorling Kindersley Book

What do spies do?

In a dark office, in an enemy country, a spy breaks open a safe. He removes the plans for a new, top-secret missile. His hands shake. He is breaking the law – risking torture and prison if the guards catch him! With a tiny camera he copies the plans. Quickly he returns the papers and silently escapes. No-one has seen him – the mission is a success!

This spy is helping to protect his country. The stolen pictures will help his country's scientists design defences against the enemy weapon. But spies do many other jobs. Some work in their home country to keep it safe from terrorists. A few are secret killers. Many more guard their own country's secrets and protect them from enemy spies.

Ancient spies at work

There have been spies since ancient times. A Bible story tells how spies sneaked into Jericho, a town in Jordan, to learn about its defences.

Spies spy for lots of different reasons. High pay attracts many of them. Others spy against their own country because they disagree with its rulers. Some spy because they have been blackmailed. They don't want to spy, but enemy spies have threatened to reveal shameful secrets unless they spy for them. Others start to spy just because they love the excitement involved. Living a secret, sometimes dangerous, life thrills them.

Many spy because they believe the information they collect on evil rulers helps make the world a safer place.

But spies don't always spy for a country. Businesses use spies, too. Just as countries try to find out their enemies plans, so companies want to know the secrets of their rivals. Industrial spying is big business. By stealing secrets from rivals, companies can make the same product at a lower price.

Spies have always had to work in secret. To help them do this, they write important messages in code. Codes turn messages into a jumble of letters that look like nonsense – hiding the original meaning. Only the sender and receiver know how to read the secret code.

Roman emperor Julius Caesar used a simple code to send messages to Rome more than 2,000 years ago. He moved each letter forward three places in the alphabet. So A became D, B became E, and so on. Written in this code, Caesar's name becomes FDHVDU.

Codes like this are simple to crack because each letter in the code stands for the same letter of the real message.

A code is like a lock – you have to find the right key. But unlike Caesar's code, modern codes are very tough to unlock.

Caesar's success in battle was partly a result of the information his spies collected about the enemy.

When the punishment for spying is death, spies will sometimes kill to avoid capture. Other spies are sent on deadly murder missions by their bosses.

Spies in 16th-century Venice killed with glass daggers. When they stabbed their victims the blade snapped off in the body, ensuring a certain death. The only clue that remained was a tiny cut.

But the deadliest killers of all were the 12th-century Japanese spies known as Ninja – "invisible men". Dressed in black, they crept silently into houses to poison or stab their unsuspecting victims.

Modern murder
Spies still kill. Bulgarian Georgi Markov was killed by a spy using a gun hidden in an umbrella. The spy shot him with a poisoned pellet.

It was said that no guard could stop a Ninja attack. One enterprising Ninja even hid in a small, dirty sewer waiting for his victim. When his victim sat on the toilet above, the Ninja killed him with a spear from below!

Wartime spies

When countries are at war, the work of spies is more important than ever. Spies try to discover everything about the enemy army – how many soldiers it has, what sort of weapons it possesses and what plans it is devising.

Spies in wartime must make sure nobody suspects them. Unlike soldiers, spies don't wear uniforms. Instead, they live, dress and talk like the enemy they are fighting against. If caught they are often executed. It is a risky business.

For John André it was a risk worth taking. In 1780, André was a British spy in the American War of Independence. He had been told that US general Benedict Arnold would surrender his fort in exchange for a lot of money.

The two men arranged a secret meeting to fix the deal. Under cover of darkness, André left his ship and got into a small boat. Draped in a large cloak, he was quickly rowed towards enemy territory.

Arnold did not arrive at the agreed time. Minutes ticked by – each one bringing André closer to dawn and the risk of capture.

At last, as dawn was approaching, Arnold appeared and the two men held their meeting. But André had waited so long he had missed the boat that was to take him back to his ship. He would have to walk through enemy lands until he was back in British-held territory.

André hid until darkness fell, then he started his dangerous journey home.

After walking many hours, he saw a British camp in the distance – he was safe! But then disaster struck! Three roving US soldiers caught André and searched him. They found secret papers which he had in his boots. The fact that he was not wearing a British uniform proved he was a spy, not a soldier, and he was shot.

Spies worked for both sides in World War II. Britain trained spies to help the French fight the German army which had invaded France. Sometimes the spies would be dropped into France by parachute at night, or set down by boats on remote beaches. All the spies wore disguises and carried false passports and documents to keep their real identities secret from the Germans. Every mission they undertook was extremely dangerous.

German troops were on the lookout for spies all the time. Spies, if caught, risked torture and even death at the hands of the Germans.

The spies helped the French resistance fighters. Together they blew up trains and bridges and helped to plan attacks on German army bases. Radio operators sent secret messages to Britain with details of German troop movements and weapons. The vital information gathered by these brave spies helped Allied troops liberate France in 1944.

German spies in World War II had a top-secret weapon called Enigma – a unique machine that turned messages 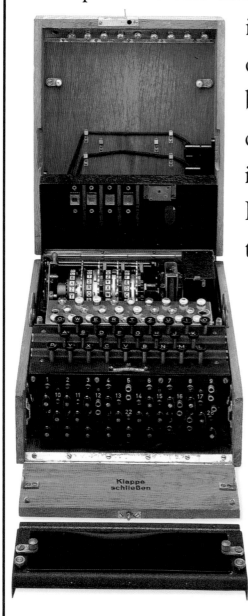 into fiendishly clever codes. The Germans believed that these codes were totally impossible to crack. Indeed, the thousands of coded messages baffled British spies for many months. The British knew it was vital to crack these German codes quickly in order to win the war.

A German Enigma machine

Beware of the Bombe
In trying to crack the codes, scientists invented the first ever electronic computer. It was called the Bombe after a type of ice-cream they ate!

Britain's top scientists went to work at Bletchley Park, the top-secret spy station, to find the key to Enigma.

At first they made little progress. Then suddenly their luck turned. An Enigma machine was captured from the Germans. Knowing how it worked would help the scientists in their efforts to crack the secret code. After months of frustratingly slow work they finally found the key!

The decoded messages proved invaluable and helped Britain and the US discover vital enemy secrets.

"Peacetime" spies

In the 1950s the world was not at war, but it was not really at peace, either. The United States feared attack by communist countries and built nuclear weapons of terrible power. They aimed the weapons at Russia and other communist countries. The communist countries were just as afraid and built similar weapons. A dangerous rivalry began.

Most countries supported either the US or Russia. People called this time of fear the Cold War. It gave spying new importance. America's spy agency, the CIA, tried to discover the strength of Russian weapons. Russia's spy agency, the KGB, sent spies on similar missions to the US. And both agencies tried to capture each other's spies.

A "mushroom" cloud after a nuclear test explosion

When the United States built the first nuclear bombs in 1945, the KGB was keen to learn the details. Russian spies were sent to the US to find out all they could.

In 1950, American couple Ethel and Julius Rosenberg were arrested for spying for the KGB. Ethel's brother worked on the bomb and gave her secrets which she then passed to the KGB. Ethel and her husband were executed for spying.

But the damage was done. The Russians had all the information they needed and had already made a nuclear bomb.

One of the worst moments in the Cold War was what became known as the Cuban Missile Crisis. In 1962, CIA spies in Cuba, a Caribbean island 150 kilometres from the US, noticed that Russian "advisors" there wore only two kinds of sports shirts. They guessed that they were soldiers in disguise. When spy planes later spotted Russian nuclear missiles on the island, World War III nearly began. Luckily the Russians backed down.

Smoking is dangerous
The CIA felt that Cuba's leader Fidel Castro was such a threat that they plotted to murder him with a poisoned cigar.

Philby and his mother

Kim Philby was a very successful spy. He worked for Britain's spy service helping to catch Russian spies. He was so respected that he was offered a job in Washington, DC, teaching spy-catching skills to the CIA. Then, in 1951, two of Philby's friends were caught spying for Russia. They escaped before agents could arrest them. Had Philby warned them? "Of course not!" he said.

But he was lying. Like his two friends, Philby was really spying for Russia. All three men were double agents, pretending to work for one side while secretly spying for the other side.

Philby carried on his treacherous and dangerous double-dealing until 1963.

Then, just as he was about to be arrested in Beirut, he disappeared. Six months later he reappeared. But this time as a KGB colonel in Russia!

Kim Philby in Russia with his new Russian wife.

The world's most famous spy, 007, works for the British Secret Service. He introduces himself with the immortal words, "My name is Bond, James Bond." He is the classic gentleman. His manners are perfect. His clothes are never creased. He drives fast, stylish cars. He is licensed to kill. And when this spy kills his enemies, he does it with style.

Bond is also famous for the unique electronic gadgets and clever cars he uses.

Bond and friend escaping

Poison pens

Like James Bond, writer Ian Fleming loved clever and dangerous gadgets. He often carried a pen that sprayed tear gas.

An ejector seat in his car sends unwanted passengers flying through the sunroof. A suitcase-sized helicopter allows him to soar over an enemy's hideaway. Even his watch hides a razor-sharp blade to cut rope.

Although James Bond is not a real spy, his creator was. During World War II, Ian Fleming worked as a spy for the British navy. Many of his own adventures were even more amazing than Bond's, and he based many of his fictional characters on people he had actually met in his years as a spy!

A spy's toolkit

All spies use clever tools to do their work. Special cameras give them sharper eyes. Hidden microphones work like super-powerful ears. Ingenious weapons and gadgets help them to escape if they are caught.

Tools and "sneakies" like these make spying much easier. However, they can also land a spy in trouble. In many countries it is forbidden to take pictures of planes, tanks or soldiers – even in peacetime. Cameras, recorders and other spying tools could arouse suspicion.

Deadly pencil

This normal-looking pencil actually conceals a sharp and deadly dagger. It could be used by spies to help fight off an enemy agent.

So these gadgets are either disguised to look like something an ordinary traveller might carry, or they are made very tiny, so a spy can easily hide them.

This may look like an ordinary briefcase – but inside is an array of secret gadgets, recorders, cameras and weapons to help make a spy's job easier.

Spies often need evidence to prove, for instance, that someone is a traitor, or that a country has a new weapon. Photos are the best evidence and spies have very special cameras. Magnifying lenses allow spies to photograph secret meetings from a long way away. Night-vision lenses turn darkness into daylight.

Soldiers wearing night-vision lenses

The view through a pair of night-vision lenses

And when an ordinary camera would make a guard suspicious, spies use tiny cameras no bigger than a matchbox.

Spy cameras first appeared more than 100 years ago. Known as "detective cameras," they were hidden in hats, watches – and even in loaves of bread!

Super snapper
During World War II this miniature camera, called a Minox, became essential equipment for all spies on active duty.

Spies may have the most up-to-date camera and possess vital details of an enemy's secrets, but pictures and notes are useless until they can be passed on to their bosses.

Today's spies can send pictures or messages by phone, fax or computer, but it wasn't always so easy. In World War I spies used birds as a secret airmail service. Pigeons flew home with letters tied to their legs or feathers!

With the invention of radio, spies no longer needed pigeons. Instead they tapped out messages on a clicking key.

Invisible ink

Spies can write in lemon juice to make a secret message. The words disappear when the juice dries – and will reappear when warmed up.

Each group of clicks signified a letter which was sent instantly, not as speech, but as short and long bursts of radio waves. These radios made communication much easier. They also made it more dangerous. Enemy agents could trace the signals straight back to the radio set – placing the operator in danger of capture.

This radio was used by British spies in World War II.

When you make a private phone call, how many people hear it? Just you and the person you are calling? Or is someone else listening too?

Tapping a phone means secretly connecting an extra phone or tape recorder to a phone line. Every time the phone is used, the conversation is automatically transmitted to a special radio receiver.

Telephone taps are not the only way of listening to a private conversation. Bugs – tiny radio sets and microphones – also pick up and transmit speech. They can be hidden anywhere around the house where two people may talk.

Pens that listen

This pen looks like any other, but it contains a tiny secret bug that can be used to listen to, and tape, a private conversation.

If a house is "bugged", a spy with a radio can hear every word that is said from the safety of a car outside!

Bug (left) shown in phone (right)

Transmitter sends speech to receiver

Light sensor

Bug picks up speech

Clips connect bug to phone line

Light sensor turns bug on when phone is lifted

Unit starts transmitter working

Bugs work on the same principle as a radio, so it is easy to tell if your home contains one of the simpler types of bugs. Just play some loud music in the suspect room and then tune a radio outside the house. When the radio is tuned to the channel the bug is using, it will play the same music you are playing in the room!

Smart bugs are much harder to find. They switch quickly between lots of channels instead of using just one. Or they spread the sounds the microphone picks up across several different channels.

Scramblers

A phone scrambler keeps calls secret. Someone with the same scrambler hears speech, but spies listening in hear only a crackle.

To detect and remove these bugs you need special scanning tools.

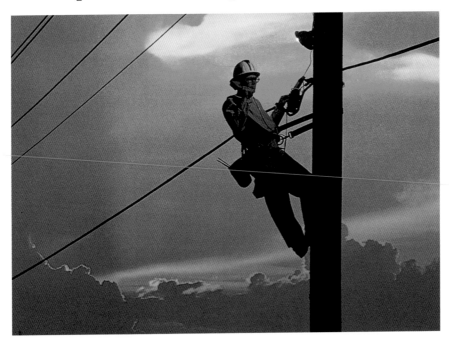

Spies can attach a bug to any part of a phone line.

Finding telephone taps is tougher still. Sometimes you can see where a spy has cut open phone wires indoors or nearby. But a spy can fit a tap to the line anywhere between the telephone and the telephone exchange, and finding it may be almost impossible.

Modern spying

Today spies continue to carry out their traditional jobs. But they are also starting to fill a new role – they are fighting crime. Spies have unique skills. They are used to gathering top-secret information. They are used to dealing with dangerous situations. They can defend themselves when they are in danger. They know how to disguise themselves so that they can move around undetected.

Spies are very good at disguise and mingling in a crowd.

Spies are helping the police to catch dangerous criminals.

These special skills can be very valuable to a country's police force. So spies are now working closely with the police in the fight against terrorists, drug smugglers and other dangerous criminals. Whoever they work for, spies have a new and powerful weapon – one that helps them secretly watch people and places from the safety of space!

Satellites are a spy's best friend. They circle high above the Earth, taking continuous pictures of everything happening below. The pictures are then transmitted to computers on the ground.

Spies can use the satellite pictures to discover important information. For instance, satellite pictures allowed US spies to locate enemy tanks and soldiers in the 1991 Gulf War.

Some satellites can even take pictures clear enough to count individual soldiers.

At one time, satellite pictures were taken on negative film. When the roll was finished, it fell back to Earth for processing – a plane flying below caught the film in mid-air! Today's modern satellites use radio signals to beam down their pictures.

This satellite image shows buildings in pink. Enlarged, you can see objects as small as a human.

Spying skills are particularly useful in the fight against drug dealers. A "spy in the sky" can locate drug fields, landing strips and drug laboratories. This information helps spies to find those who harvest and transport the drugs. Once enough evidence has been gathered, the police can arrest those involved.

Spies also help police track and catch organized-crime gangs. They often go under cover and become members of a group, reporting back to the police on the organization's plans. Information such as how the gang obtains its weapons can help the police defeat the illegal arms trade.

Spies in the CIA work closely with their police counterparts to help combat terrorism in the US. and other countries. For instance, they helped to capture the terrorists who bombed New York's World Trade Centre in 1993.

Terror tactics
Around the world, police and spies work together to try to stop terrorists from planting deadly bombs like this one.

Although spies may be helping police beat drug dealers and terrorists, they still have to make sure their own secrets are safe – as one recent case proves.

Aldrich Ames worked for the CIA, where he was in charge of catching Russian spies. In 1985 he was put to work to uncover a double agent who had sold the KGB the name of every American spy in Russia. But as time went by, doubts about Ames began to grow. Why couldn't he catch the double agent?

Aldrich Ames when he was first arrested

Aldrich Ames on his way to serving a life sentence

CIA chiefs grew suspicious of his lack of success and ordered him to be followed. They filmed him taking top-secret papers and hiding them in hollow trees where Russian spies exchanged the papers for piles of money. Aldrich Ames was the double agent! His double-dealing had made him rich. The American spies he named for money were less lucky. They were executed.

Many of today's spies don't even have to leave home. Instead of travelling overseas, they can turn on a computer and the Internet links them to millions of other computers all around the world.

China has already trained its top spies to wage war with computer viruses.

Every two minutes someone uses the Internet to try to connect to the Pentagon – the US war office. Most of these "attacks" are totally harmless, but not all of them.

Schoolboy spy
A "spy" who broke into US Air Force computers turned out to be Richard Pryce, a brilliant 16-year-old from Britain.

During the war in former Yugoslavia, Serbian computer experts attacked NATO's computers by flooding them with e-mail messages. The damage was repaired but, in the future, this kind of warfare on the Internet could do as much harm as bombs and bullets.

Glossary

American War of Independence
The war (1776–83) that Americans fought to end British rule in their country.

Blackmail
Using an embarrassing secret to force someone to do something they don't want to do.

Bugs
Tiny listening devices that allow spies in another place to hear conversations in the room where the bug is hidden.

CIA
Central Intelligence Agency, the spy agency of the USA.

Code
A secret way of writing a message to hide its meaning.

Computer virus
A harmful program that spreads from computer to computer.

Disguise
Any way of changing peoples' identity to stop others from recognizing them.

Double agents
People who pretend to spy for one country while really spying for another country.

Internet
World-wide network of computers used for trade, to provide information and to send messages.

KGB
The spy agency of the Soviet Union (now Russia).

NATO
North Atlantic Treaty Organization.

Night-vision lenses
Lenses that enable the wearer to see in the dark.

Ninjas
Secret killer spies who stalked Japan eight centuries ago.

Nuclear weapons
Bombs that use radioactive materials to create explosions of enormous destructive power.

Radio waves
Invisible rays that carry sound to distant places.

Resistance fighters
People who secretly fight against the enemy soldiers who have invaded their country.

Satellites
Spacecraft that constantly circle above the Earth, often taking photographs of the land below.

Surrender
To voluntarily stop fighting and give up to your enemies.

Taps
Electronic devices fitted into a phone or a phone line that allow spies to listen to private telephone calls.

Terrorists
People who seek to force others to do things by frightening them with acts or threats of violence.

Torture
Purposefully causing someone pain to try to make them give away a secret.